Contents

Sorting solid shapes   4

Building with solid shapes   6

Sorting flat shapes   8

Pictures with flat shapes   10

Matching solid shapes   12

Making patterns   14

Symmetry   16

Position   18

Direction and movement   20

Supporting notes for adults   22

Suggestions for using this book 24

Sorting solid shapes

Look at the shapes in the picture.
Name them.

sphere

cone

Point to a shape which is not a cone.

4

cube

pyramid

Challenge

Use a set of
shapes to make
a model.
Can you name
the shapes
that you used?

Building with solid shapes

Look at the picture.
Name the shapes.

Get some solid shapes.
Copy the picture with your shapes.

Sorting flat shapes

Look at the shapes in the picture.
Name them.

square   rectangle

Point to a shape that is not a rectangle.
What shape did you choose?

circle   triangle   star

Challenge
Look around the room.
Can you find these shapes
in things in the room?

9

Pictures with flat shapes

Get some flat shapes.

Copy the picture with the shapes.

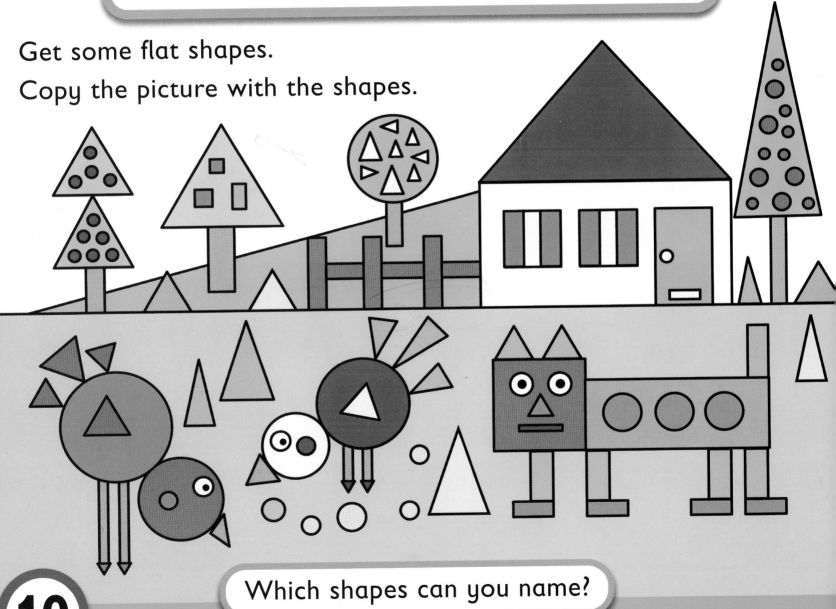

10

Which shapes can you name?

Challenge

Get some flat shapes. Make your own picture with the shapes. Can you draw your picture?

Matching solid shapes

Which shape made each print?

Can you name all the things in the picture?

Challenge

Get some damp sand.
Find some solid shapes.
Look carefully at the faces
of the shapes.
Decide what print it will make.
Now print in the sand.

13

Making patterns

Say the patterns in each row.

Get some paper and crayons. Choose one of the patterns. Copy it on paper. What will come next in the pattern? And next? Draw this on paper.

14

15

Symmetry

Get a small safety mirror.

Put the mirror on the center line of the cat.

Look in the mirror. What can you see?

Now try the other pictures.

center

Use the mirror. Put it on the pictures like this. What can you see in the mirror?

Fold a sheet of paper in half. Draw a shape and cut it out. Be careful not to cut away the fold. What do you think you will see when you open the paper?

Position

Who is sitting under the table?

What can you see on top of the table?

Where is the ball?

What can you see on the shelf?

Challenge

Paint a picture of you.
Now paint a cat next to you.
What else could you put in
your picture?

19

Direction and movement

Help the animals get home.

Can you find another way to send the dog home?

Challenge

Find some things in the room that turn.

Supporting notes for adults

Sorting solid shapes – pages 4-5

Read the shape labels to the children as they point to the mathematical shapes at the top of the pages. Encourage them to find examples of each shape in the picture.

Building with solid shapes – pages 6-7

If the children find it difficult to make the shapes in the picture, start with the house. Ask the children to match the shapes to the house, then build it. They will need a cube and a pyramid for this.

Sorting flat shapes – pages 8-9

Encourage the children to say the name of each shape as you read the label and to point to the mathematical shapes at the top of the pages. Encourage them to find each shape in the picture.

Pictures with flat shapes – pages 10-11

Have the children make each item in the picture. Encourage them to find the shape cutouts they will need, and to name these before they start to make their picture.

Matching solid shapes – pages 12-13

The picture includes some everyday items as well as mathematical shapes. Begin with the shell, the footprints... and discuss what could have made these imprints before looking at the mathematical shapes and their imprints.

Making patterns – pages 14-15

Have the children say what the images are in each sequence such as cat, bird, butterfly, cat, bird, butterfly. Encourage them to repeat this as you point to each image in turn.

Symmetry – pages 16-17

Encourage the children to guess what the whole picture will be before they check with the mirror.

Position – pages 18-19

Ask the children questions such as, "What is on top... under... beside the...?"

Direction and movement – pages 20-21

Encourage the children to talk about the route that they chose and to describe the directions. At this stage, they will probably find "left" and "right" difficult to remember, so help them by supplying the correct word and pointing along the line of movement on the maze.

Suggestions for using this book

Children will enjoy looking through the book and talking about the colorful pictures. Sit somewhere comfortable together. Read the instructions to the children, then encourage them to take part in the activity and check whether they understand what to do.

The activities encourage children to use shapes to make buildings, patterns, and pictures so that they learn more about the properties of the shapes. Encourage them to talk about what they have done, what worked well in their model or picture, and why, and how it could be improved. In this way, they will extend their understanding of the properties of the shapes.

The connection between solid shapes and flat ones is very important for children to understand. Encourage children to make prints from solid shapes and to describe what they can see. For example, pressing one face of a box into damp sand will leave a rectangular imprint. Now ask the children to describe and name that face of the box.

Children are introduced to the idea of symmetry. It is really useful to have a mirror handy for these activities. Show the children how to place the mirror along the mirror line of the picture and then to see the reflection in the mirror and how it connects to the picture on the page.

Help the children extend their understanding of the vocabulary for position, direction, and movement by playing guessing games such as "I Spy," for describing where things are, and "Simon Says," for movement and directions. They will show you by their responses whether or not they understand the vocabulary used.

Copyright © QEB Publishing 2004

First published in the United States by
QEB Publishing, Inc.
23062 La Cadena Drive
Laguna Hills
CA 92653

This edition published by
Teacher Created Resources, Inc.
6421 Industry Way
Westminster, CA 92683

www.teachercreated.com

Library of Congress Control Number: 2004102072

ISBN 1-4206-8170-2

Written by Ann Montague-Smith
Designed and edited by The Complete Works
Illustrated by Jenny Tulip
Photography by Steve Lumb and Michael Wicks

Creative Director Louise Morley
Editorial Manager Jean Coppendale

Printed and bound in China

With thanks to:

Read · Think · Do

MATH

Ages 5 & Up

Sizes and Shapes
Book 2

Ann Montague-Smith

Teacher Created Resources